Contents

Getting started

3. How to use my journal..................☐
5. Reflection ....☐
6. Our Essential Agreements ....☐
8. My learner profile........................☐
10. Reflecting on the learner profile....☐
12. Exploring learner profile
    attributes..................................☐

Self-management

13. Mindfulness................................☐
14. Noticing feelings in my body ....☐
15. Managing my emotions ....☐
16. Reflecting on my emotions ....☐
18. Using strategies to manage my
    emotions ....☐
20. Taking action..............................☐
21. Perseverance...............................☐
22. Taking action..............................☐

Social skills

23. Social-emotional intelligence..........☐
24. Being aware of myself ....☐
25. Recognizing feelings
    and emotions ....☐

26. Understanding responsibility..........☐
27. Recognizing and taking
    responsibility.............................☐
28. Using strategies to
    resolve conflict..........................☐
29. Taking action ....☐
30. Interpersonal relationships ....☐
31. Supporting success
    through co-operation....................☐
32. Encouraging group collaboration....☐
33. Taking action.............................☐
34. What is taking action?..................☐

Thinking skills

36. Recording thinking and progress....☐
37. Taking action ....☐
38. Critical thinking ....☐
40. Creative thinking ....☐
41. Critical and creative thinking ....☐
42. Taking action ....☐
43. Transfer: metacognition ....☐
44. Transfer....................................☐

Research skills

46. Information literacy .... ☐
47. Conceptual questions .... ☐
48. Understanding the steps to planning research .... ☐
50. Media literacy .... ☐
51. Identifying reliable and unreliable sources .... ☐
52. Choosing research tools .... ☐
53. Using media to gather information .... ☐
54. Ethical use of media literacy .... ☐
55. Understanding the responsibilities of digital citizenship .... ☐
56. Contributing responsibly to digital platforms .... ☐
57. Taking action .... ☐

Communication skills

58. Exchanging information .... ☐
59. Talking and listening .... ☐
60. Expressing ideas and opinions .... ☐
61. Understanding perspective in a multi-cultural world .... ☐
62. ICT: forms of communication .... ☐
63. Communicating using different forms of media .... ☐
64. Using technology to share information .... ☐
65. Literacy .... ☐
66. Organizing information .... ☐
68. Understanding the function of writing .... ☐
70. Taking action .... ☐

Sustainable Development Goals

71. Taking action: the SDGs .... ☐
76. Taking action .... ☐
77. Reflecting on my year .... ☐
79. What's next? .... ☐
80. Feelings in my body .... ☐

How to use my journal

Welcome

This is your journal. Please use it to draw or write your ideas and thoughts.

There are no right or wrong answers – be free to explore.

Reflection helps us to develop an awareness of ourselves and others.

Reflection can be …

1. **Being aware** of the present.
   Describing your feelings.

2. **Wondering.**
   Giving your perspective. Making connections.

3. **Thinking** back on your day.
   Thinking forward about how to improve.

4. **Planning** goals for yourself and next steps.
   Planning how to apply your skills to take action.

> Reflection involves all the **essential elements** (perhaps not all at the same time!)
> - Knowledge
> - Concepts
> - Skills
> - Learner profile
> - Action

Use the activities in this journal to support your inquiries and to:

- develop your **thinking skills**
- reflect on and develop your **learner profile attributes**
- assess your **approaches to learning** skills
- set **SMART** goals (see page 4)
- consider your **progress**
- **take action**!

3

How to use my journal

The five **approaches to learning** are:

Self-management skills – Be organized and manage your different states of mind.

Social skills – Understand other people and how to work together.

Thinking skills – Be critical and creative, think about how we think, and understand how we can use what we have learned to help us with new learning.

Research skills – Use different methods to find information and understand how to use media safely and responsibly.

Communication skills – Exchange information using different forms of literacy and Information and Communication Technology (ICT).

> **SMART** goals
>
> **S**pecific: Be clear about what you want to do. Answer the questions: Who? What? Where? Why? Which?
>
> **M**easurable: Set a goal you can measure (How much? How many?).
>
> **A**ttainable: Aim to do something that's not too hard (or too easy).
>
> **R**elevant: Keep your goal related to what you want in the future.
>
> **T**ime: Decide when you will achieve your goal (and try to stick to it).

Here are two ways to record your reflections:

What other ways could you try?

Reflection

If you could do or be anything for one day, what would you choose?

What three things can you do to meet this goal?

1. ....
2. ....
3. ....

What you have just done is **reflective thinking**.

goal setting thinking of goals we want to achieve
reflection thinking about our strengths, our challenges and where we want to be

5

Our Essential Agreements

Creating essential agreements helps us to have a positive classroom where we can all learn and feel happy.

Reflect on these questions.

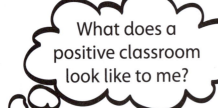

What does a positive classroom look like to me?

What routines help my learning?

How would I like to be treated?

Discuss with your classmates and record your ideas.

What agreements would you like to have?
Write and draw your ideas.

 How do your ideas compare with your classmates' ideas?

My learner profile

What sort of a learner are you? Some of us are more curious; others are more balanced.

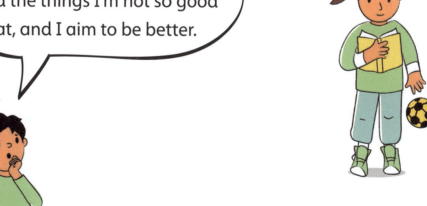

Reflecting on the learner profile

1 William Kamkwamba was born in 1987 in Malawi, Africa.

2 While William was young, the country experienced famine and his family couldn't afford to send him to school.

3 One day, William found a book called *Using Energy* in the library. This book taught him all about windmills.

4 When he was just 14 years old, William decided to build his own windmill using parts people had thrown away.

The most difficult part to find was the generator, but William was clever and used a dynamo from a bicycle. The windmill worked!

1987
William is born

2002
William finds *Using Energy* and builds a working windmill

 What learner profile attributes does William show?
Does William show different attributes at different times?

10

5 Another of William's inventions was a solar-powered water pump that supplied the first drinking water to his village.

6 William wrote a book telling his story, called *The Boy Who Harnessed the Wind.*

7 In 2010, William won the GO Ingenuity Award. He used the money to run classes in his village, teaching young people to make wind turbines and repair water pumps.

8 William is now celebrated as an inventor, engineer and author who improved the lives of many through his inventions.

2007	2009	2010	Today
William builds a solar-powered water pump	William publishes *The Boy Who Harnessed the Wind*	William wins the GO Ingenuity Award and sets up classes	

dynamo a type of generator
famine a shortage of food that causes many people to die
generator a machine that uses movement to make electrical energy
harnessed got control of and used
pump a machine that forces water to move
turbines machines that use air or water to make power

11

Exploring learner profile attributes

Which learner profile attributes do you show?
Do you show some more than others?
Create a pie chart of the attributes you show.

My learner profile

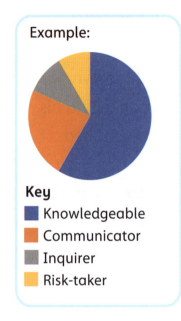

Example:

Key
- Knowledgeable
- Communicator
- Inquirer
- Risk-taker

Key

 Share your results with a partner. Compare, contrast and discuss.

 Which areas might you need to develop further?

Mindfulness

We feel emotions in different parts of our body. Practising mindfulness can make us aware of the connections between the mind and the body.

Reflect on the pictures.

What emotions might this child be feeling? How do you know?

Where in the body might we feel this emotion? What does it feel like?

When might we feel this way?

How does your body language show what you're feeling?
Use words or pictures to explain.

Emotions:
afraid
confused
excited
happy
sad
surprised
worried

13

Noticing feelings in my body

You are going to do a mindfulness practice. Lie down and listen to your teacher read 'Feelings in my body'.

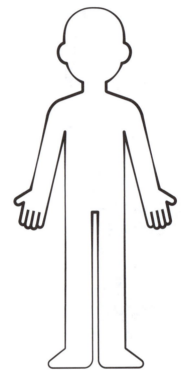

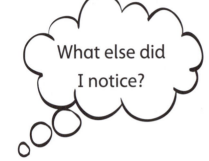

What emotion did I feel?

What else did I notice?

Where in my body did I feel it?

What colour would it be?

Colour to show where you felt the emotion.

Being mindful of feelings in my body will help me ....

14

Managing my emotions

Our breath is a powerful tool that can help us manage big emotions like fear, worry, anger or sadness. It also helps us to focus.

Try the 'Five finger breathing technique' to focus on your breath for one minute.

First, reflect on this question.

1. Spread your fingers wide.

2. Place a finger from your other hand at the base of your thumb.

3. Breathe in as you slowly run your finger up your thumb.

4. Breathe out, running your finger down the other side.

5. Repeat on each finger.

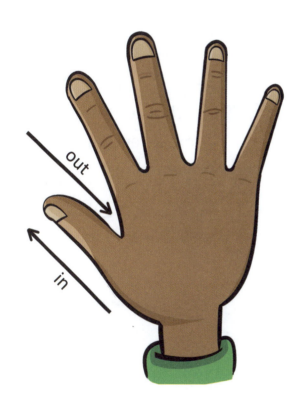

Now reflect on these questions.

15

Reflecting on my emotions

What big emotions can you think of?

16

Which learner profile attributes might help you manage big emotions?

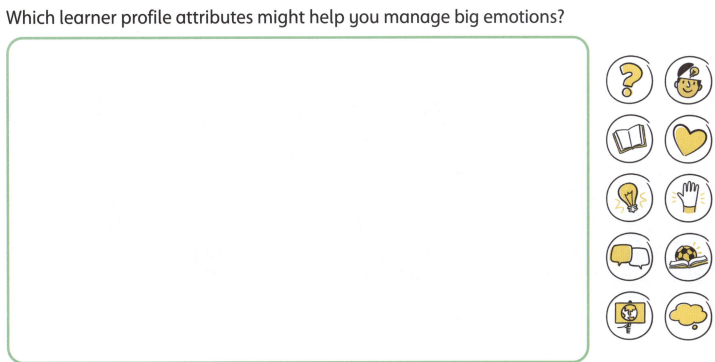

Using strategies to manage my emotions

When we are feeling big emotions like fear, worry, anger or sadness, it can be helpful to have tools and strategies to help.

Colour-code these strategies.
Green = I like this.
Orange = I would try this.
Red = This isn't for me.

Draw ☐

Go outside ☐

Listen to music ☐

Read ☐

Take deep breaths ☐

Go for a walk ☐

Be with friends ☐

With a partner, research different tools and strategies for managing big emotions. Draw or write about them.

Which idea do I like best?

Is there an idea that might not work? Why not?

 Share your ideas with the class.

Taking action

Choose one tool or strategy to help you manage your emotions.
Draw it here.

Who could you share this tool or strategy with?
Parents or carers? Family? Friends? Your learning community?

Perseverance

Sometimes we feel frustrated and we want to give up. We might think:

Perseverance means working hard to achieve something, even when it gets difficult.
- Think of a goal you have.
- Draw an arrow on the line to show how close you are to achieving the goal.
- Where will your arrow be if you use perseverance?

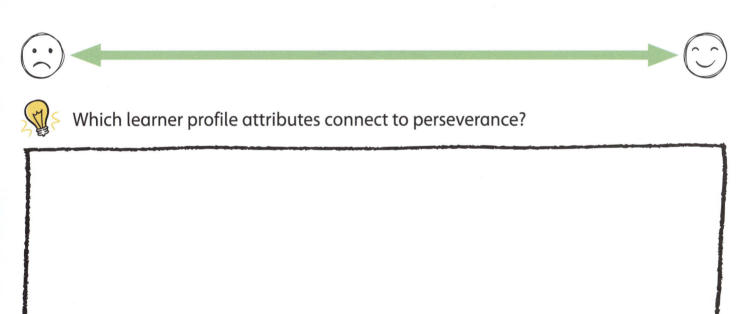

Which learner profile attributes connect to perseverance?

Taking action

Often, taking action is not easy. Here are some people who persevered.

Melati and Isabel Wijsen

Nelson Mandela

William Kamkwamba

"We've been working to reduce plastic pollution for over 10 years!"

"It always seems impossible until it's done."

"Even though I couldn't go to school, I kept learning in the library."

When have you persevered?

Social-emotional intelligence

When we are aware of ourselves and think about how we might affect other people, we have social-emotional intelligence.

Draw yourself. Then write about yourself.
What makes you unique (special)?

Words you could use:

brave	kind
creative	fun
friendly	thoughtful

23

Being aware of myself

- ☐ Fill this empty jar with things that make you happy.
- ☐ You can draw, write or stick pictures.
- ☐ You can come back to it and add more at any time.

> "Knowing yourself is the beginning of all wisdom."
> *Aristotle*

What might others know, understand or think about you, based on your jar?

....

....

Recognizing feelings and emotions

Reflect on the last few weeks. When were you …

Excited	
Proud	
Scared	
Struggling with something difficult	
Laughing at something funny	

 What might someone learn about you from these reflections?

Understanding responsibility

What does being responsible mean to you?

Work with a partner. Think of examples when you've been or felt responsible.

I have jobs that people expect me to complete.

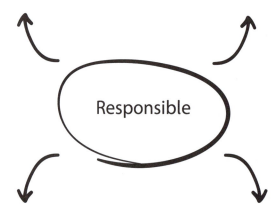

Responsible

 In what ways do you have a responsibility to other people, or to the world?

Recognizing and taking responsibility

Look carefully at the image below. What do you see, think, wonder? Write your thoughts around the image.

 Now, consider **your** role in bullying. How do your actions impact your life? How might your actions affect others? Are you being principled? You do **not** have to share your thoughts with anyone else.

27

Using strategies to resolve conflict

Reflect on how you have resolved conflict in the past.
What worked well for you? What didn't work as well?
What behaviour might you see from 'peace breakers' (people who cause conflict)?
What behaviour might you see from 'peace makers' (people who resolve conflict)?

Peace <u>breakers</u>	Peace <u>makers</u>
Speak when others are speaking	Use kind words

 Discuss your answers with a partner.

conflict an argument or fight
resolve find a solution

28

Taking action

How could you use peace-making skills to make the world a better place?

Which Sustainable Development Goals (SDGs) connect with your ideas? (See pages 71–75.)

Interpersonal relationships

Collaboration and co-operation are part of working together as a team. We share ideas, listen to others, help each other and solve problems.

Problem

Solved

What does collaboration look like to you?

Supporting success through co-operation

Draw some people you work with in a group (classmates, adults who help, community members).

Think about how they make your group stronger. List two ways they are amazing!

Name: .... Name: .... Name: ....

1. .... 1. .... 1. ....

2. .... 2. .... 2. ....

What might help the group succeed?	What might get in the way?
good communication	

31

Encouraging group collaboration

Work in a group and discuss how you could resolve these situations.
How can you make it a positive experience for everyone?

Problem	Questions
You suggest a great idea for your group. No one else thinks it is a great idea. You feel angry and hurt.	Why do you feel this way? How could you put your hurt to one side and carry on working together?

Solutions

Problem	Questions
A person in your group refuses to do what the rest of the team has suggested.	How could you solve this problem? What skills would you all need to focus on with this problem?

Solutions

 How easy do you find working with others?
How could understanding yourself help when you are collaborating?

32

Taking action

You have learned how building positive relationships is an important skill. How could you use these skills to take action?

> "Every one of us must do our part. Together, let's create a healthy planet and a safer future for us all."
>
> *UN.org*

33

What is taking action?

- ☐ Consider the action categories:

    Participation – Working with others

    Advocacy – Speaking up for others

- ☐ Write your ideas for personal, community and global action.
- ☐ Show or describe what action might look like for yourself or others.

What might action look like?
Personal action What personal action do I want to take?

34

What might action look like?

Community action

What could I do for my local community?

Global action

How can I connect to the SDGs?

Recording thinking and progress

When have you been successful this week?
What do you need to do to be successful?
It's helpful to break it down into stages.

I know I will be successful if ...

What do I want to know, understand and do?	What would success look like?	How could I make a positive change for myself or others?

 How could you record your progress?

36

Taking action

List your top three goals for this year.

1. ....

2. ....

3. ....

Choose one of your goals. What action steps will you take this week to help you to reach it?

Step 1

Step 2

Step 3

Step 4

Critical thinking

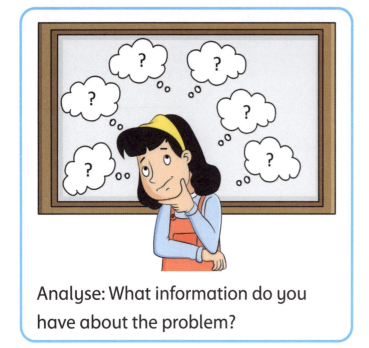

Analyse: What information do you have about the problem?

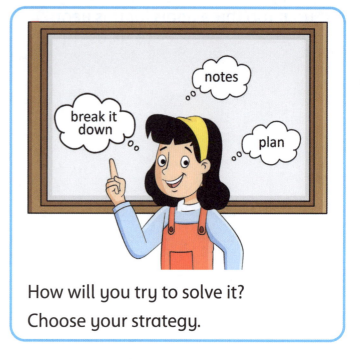

How will you try to solve it? Choose your strategy.

In a group, try these two different strategies for looking at a problem.

1 Note your thinking.

This is not a hat

2 See-think-wonder

Be aware of your metacognition (the different ways you think). Write your ideas in the table about what you see, think and wonder when you look at this image.

See	Think	Wonder

Reflect on which strategy you prefer.

I prefer strategy .... because ....

....

....

39

Creative thinking

What kind of learner are you?

a risk-taker, confident, brave

caring, co-operative, gentle, patient

☐ Reflect on what kind of learner you are.
☐ Are you more like the lion or the mouse?
☐ Choose two learner profile attributes to describe yourself.

Learner profile attribute:

Learner profile attribute:

 Share your reflections with a partner.
What makes you both unique? What attributes do you share?

Critical and creative thinking

Think about being a global thinker and about international mindedness.
Write definitions of them.

Global thinker	International mindedness

How do you think your two definitions could be connected? Or not connected?

....

....

....

....

....

....

Reflect on how you have used critical and creative thinking skills in class.

41

Taking action

Think of a big problem that you've heard about.

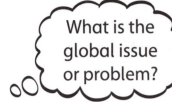 What is the global issue or problem?

 How does it impact the present?

How might it impact the future?

How could you begin to solve this problem? What creative ideas can you come up with?

Transfer: metacognition

Being aware of how our minds work allows us to be more **reflective**. It helps us see how one way of thinking might be useful when learning something new.

Complete the table.

What do I already know about our current unit of inquiry?	What do I hope to learn from our current unit of inquiry?

How are you an inquirer?

....

....

How are you knowledgeable?

....

....

Transfer

When you start something new, think about how you learned something before.

Talk to a partner about what you gained from your last inquiry.

How could these transfer skills help with your new inquiry?

....

....

....

....

What knowledge and skills from your last inquiry will you transfer to your new inquiry? Add them into the jars.

Reflect on how transfer skills did or did not help with your learning.

....

....

....

....

....

Information literacy

Information literacy is having the knowledge and skills to find information and to decide if that information is useful.

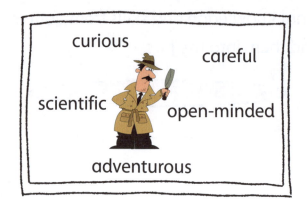

Reflect on your research skills.
What does it mean to be an inquirer?

How do you feel when you are asked to do research? Why?

 What do you still wonder about research?

Conceptual questions

Being curious leads us down new paths of discovery.

What are you most curious about?
Reflect on these themes and write your questions below.

Understanding the steps to planning research

Work in a group. Discuss the journey of a researcher.
How might the map lead you to the treasure of new knowledge?

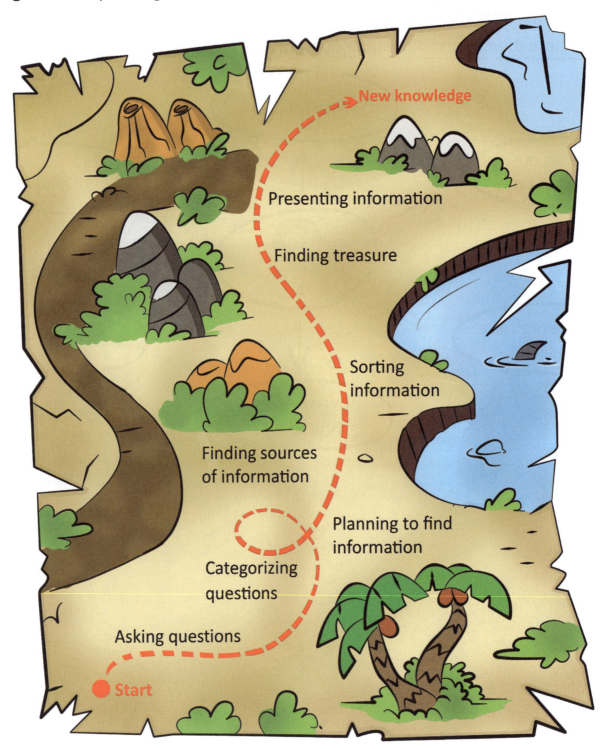

categorizing dividing into sets or groups

Consider your current inquiry. Create your own treasure map showing the route to find answers to your inquiry.

What is the first thing you will do?
What do you want to know?
What challenges might you face?
What do you expect to find?

Media literacy

Record your thoughts on this quote below, then discuss with a partner.
What conclusions did you come to?

"You can't always believe everything you read online."

Abraham Lincoln, 1861

My thoughts:

My partner's thoughts:

How could the skill of **media literacy** help your research?

media literacy being able to find and use different forms of media

50

Identifying reliable and unreliable sources

Read and reflect on this source of information.

The wild hairy haggis, a shy animal from Scotland, is Britain's latest animal to join the endangered list. Recent data from some school children suggests that the wild hairy haggis is facing many dangers, leading the local postman to classify it as endangered. The animal's special features include a coat of fur and legs of different lengths, making it well adapted to running around the mountains it calls home. These animals are believed to live in the most remote and hard to reach regions of Scotland, making it difficult to study them and protect their small populations.

Discuss why you think it may or may not be reliable.
Record your thoughts in the red box (unreliable) and green box (reliable).

Unreliable

Reliable

adapted suited to the place where it lives
classify to put things in groups

endangered in danger of not existing in the future

 Create some top tips for identifying reliable and unreliable sources of information.

Choosing research tools

Consider your inquiry. Where did you go to find answers to your questions?

Local information **Global information**

What did you use to answer your questions? (Books, websites, interviews, surveys, experiments, maps ...)

Record your reflections below.

Which sources of information did you use that surprised you?

Which objects or tools helped your inquiry?

How could you improve this research journey next time?

Using media to gather information

Good researchers use more than one source to gather, compare and evaluate information. We can find a range of perspectives when we use different media sources.

Consider your inquiry. What are you trying to find out?

Open questions:
　Why …
　What if …
　How might …

These may lead to other questions and can have more than one answer.

Closed questions:
　Did …
　Will …
　Who …

What problem do I want to solve?	What questions do I have?	Where might I find the answers? Who or what might help me?

Ethical use of media literacy

Using media **ethically** creates a safe and happy environment for everyone to enjoy.

Be responsible and kind when using media. Follow the rules and respect other users.

Be honest and check with an adult if you're not sure about something you see or hear.

Be balanced and don't use technology too much.

How confident do you feel about safety and responsibility when you are researching? Colour the blocks, starting from the left, to show how confident you feel.

I feel uncomfortable and need lots of help.

I am very confident and can teach others too.

Explain your choice. Why do you feel that way?

....

....

....

....

ethically doing something in a way that's correct and fair

54

Understanding the responsibilities of digital citizenship

- ☐ What are the responsibilities of a digital citizen?
- ☐ What are the best rules to follow when you are using the internet?
- ☐ How can you stay safe, respect others and protect intellectual property?

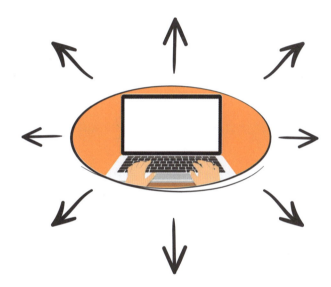

citizenship your rights and duties as part of a community
intellectual property an idea or invention that belongs to someone

55

Contributing responsibly to digital platforms

All good digital citizens respect themselves and others, protect privacy and copyright, and stay safe online.

Complete the text boxes with your responses to the following messages.

Can you send me Gino's address please so I can share it?

We need to post our group photos on our website.

Don't speak to Clara any more. She was mean to me.

- Share your ideas with a partner. How did you each respond?
- What suggestions could you give your partner about digital responsibility?

privacy a person's right not to share their own information
copyright control of a piece of work so that others cannot copy it

Taking action

Reflect on the skills you've been developing.

- Working with media to create ideas and apply information
- Understanding and applying the ethical use of technology
- Planning, researching and presenting information

How could you use these skills to help yourself?

How could you use these skills to help others?

Exchanging information

Exchanging information is how we communicate ideas, feelings, opinions and concerns. It is far more than simply talking and listening.

- ☐ How do these pictures show **communication** skills?
- ☐ What forms of communication can you identify?

Reflect on your communication skills.

I'm a confident communicator when I …

I find communication difficult when …

I'd like to improve my communication in these areas …

Talking and listening

Think about the different ways that we communicate with each other.
List as many forms of communication as you can think of.

Exchange information by talking and listening.
- ☐ Tell a partner your preferred forms of communication and listen to their ideas.
- ☐ Share your thoughts with your classmates.

Think	Pair	Share and compare
I think …	My partner thinks …	My classmates think …

Expressing ideas and opinions

1 Let's start a conversation!
Tick to show if you agree or disagree with these statements.

Opinion	Agree ✓	Disagree ✓
All children should have a pet.		
Everyone should have the day off school or work on their birthday.		
If people refuse to recycle their waste, they should have to pay money.		

2 Discuss your opinions in a group.
Use these ideas to structure your argument.

Setting out your argument
- First of all, …
- I think … because …
- I'd like to begin by saying …
- Let's start with this …

Discussing and responding
- In my opinion … because …
- I agree with … because …
- I believe … because …
- I disagree with … because …

Concluding
- I'd like to add to … because …
- Finally, …
- In conclusion, …
- In summary, …

 What did you hear others say that was useful?

60

Understanding perspective in a multi-cultural world

Consider the two worlds.

What would it be like if everyone spoke the same language?

ICT: forms of communication

There are many different forms of communication, and we can choose those that work best for delivering our message.

What forms of communication have you used in the past? How did you use them? How do you feel about trying new forms of communication?

Communicating using different forms of media

- ☐ Create a list of forms of communication you would like to try.
- ☐ Add a tick box next to each idea. Once you have used that form of communication, you can tick it off.

Using technology to share information

We have many forms of technology to help deliver our message in the best possible way to our audience.

- ☐ Reflect on what you have been learning.
- ☐ How could you best present your knowledge?
- ☐ How can technology support your presentation?
- ☐ What will you use/need?

What I **know**	What I **need**	**Action** I will take

64

Literacy

Record all of the ways you use reading and writing as a means of communication.

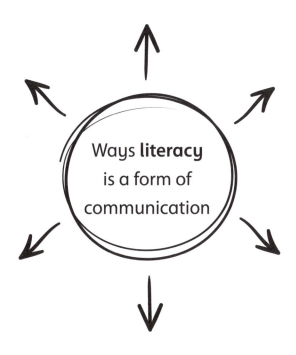

 How do you feel about **literacy** as a form of communication?

literacy being able to read, write, speak, listen and communicate

Organizing information

Analyse each of these ways of organizing information. Record your thoughts around each one.

1. Mind map

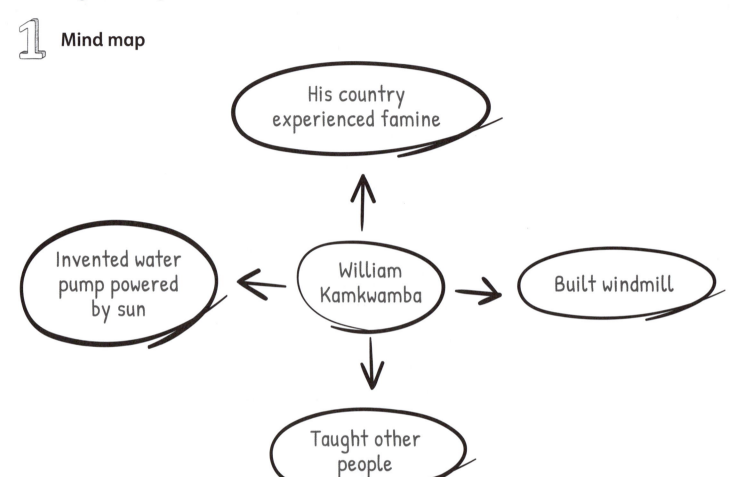

2. Bullet points

William Kamkwamba
- Born in Malawi, Africa – 1987
- No school
- Read library book Using Energy
- Built windmill
- Invented solar-powered water pump

Table

Problem	not enough food energy expensive
What did William do to solve it?	built windmill invented solar-powered water pump taught young people to make and repair pumps and windmills

 Paraphrasing

While William was young, the country experienced famine and his family couldn't afford to send him to school. One day, William found a book called *Using Energy* in the library. This book taught him all about windmills.

After William stopped going to school during a famine, he read a book called Using Energy that taught him about windmills.

 Decide which ways of organizing information you will use in the future. Explain why you chose them and how they will help your communication skills.

67

Understanding the function of writing

☐ Think about the best ways to persuade, inform and entertain people.
☐ What forms of writing would be best for these three purposes? Record your ideas below.
☐ Refer back to this list when you are planning your presentations.

Persuade	Inform	Entertain
To convince others of a certain point of view	To teach or give information to others	To hold the attention of the audience through enjoyment

What forms of writing have you used recently?
What was the purpose of this writing?

 Discuss your ideas with a partner.
Do you think you chose the right form for the audience?
What worked well and what could you improve?

Taking action

Consider your inquiry. Where might you want to take action?

Participation
Work with others.

Advocacy
Speak up for others.

Social justice
Support equal rights.

Lifestyle choices
Make good choices.

Social entrepreneurship
Create a business to help people.

 How could your communication skills be put into practice?

Taking action: the SDGs

There are 17 Sustainable Development Goals that we are all working together to achieve. 'Sustainable' means using natural resources in a way that we could keep doing for a long time.

Affordable and clean energy

We must make sure that everyone has access to energy. We must also continue to develop renewable energy sources like wind and solar.

What do we need energy for? What do you wonder?

71

Taking action: the SDGs

Decent work and economic growth

Everyone should have opportunities for work that pays fairly. These jobs should also help the country's economy to grow.

Draw yourself in the job you might want to do when you're older.

Industry, innovation and infrastructure

Industry is a group that makes things.

Innovation is creating new things that solve problems or improve things.

Infrastructure is things like transport and communications.

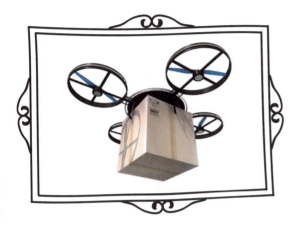

Be an innovator!

Think of a problem you have faced. What could you create to solve it?

Draw your invention here.

 Why is creative thinking important to the SDGs?

Taking action: the SDGs

Reduced inequalities

Everyone should be treated equally, and we should all have access to the same opportunities.

Around the world, 122 million girls do not have access to education. What do you wonder?

Sustainable cities and communities

We must use resources carefully to make sure they don't run out in the future.

What could you do to make your town or city more sustainable?

Taking action

We can transfer what we have learned from our research to take action for ourselves and for others.

- ☐ Reflect on your unit of inquiry.
- ☐ Who might benefit from your research?
- ☐ How could you use your research to take action?
- ☐ Record your ideas around the images.

You: being happy and healthy

Our natural world

Local community

People around the world

The United Nations SDGs:

Reflecting on my year

Something I learned …

Something I am proud of …

The SDG I thought about the most was …

The learner profile attribute that I used the most was …

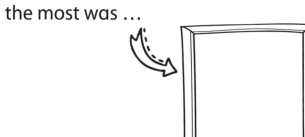

Reflecting on my year

The book I loved the most was about …

....
....
....
....

A memory I'll keep …

....
....
....
....

This is a drawing of …

....
....
....
....
....

What's next?

Next year, I hope to …

Feelings in my body

Lie down and make yourself comfortable. You can close your eyes if you like. Start by taking a few deep breaths at your own speed.

Today, we are going to notice where different feelings are felt in our bodies.

Start by thinking of a time when you felt really happy.

Where were you? Who were you with? What did you do?

How does it feel when you think about this happy time? How does it feel in your body? Where in your body do you feel it? Can you feel happiness in your stomach? Or in your heart? Maybe in your head or face? Just notice where you feel happy in your body. Does the feeling have a colour? If so, what colour is happy?

Now see if you can think about a time when you were really angry or upset.

Where were you? What happened?

How does it feel when you think about this time when you were angry? How does it feel in your body? Where in your body do you feel it? Maybe in your chest? Your shoulders? Your face? Or somewhere else?

Does the feeling have a colour? If so, what colour is angry?

Think of a time when you felt excited.

Where were you? Who were you with? What were you doing?

How does it feel when you think about this time when you felt excited? How does it feel in your body? Where in your body do you feel it? Maybe in your arms? Your legs? Your stomach? Or somewhere else? Where in your body do you feel excited?

Does the feeling have a colour? If so, what colour is excited?

Soon this exercise will be over, and I'll ask you to open your eyes. Keep your eyes closed until I tell you.

Open your eyes now.